BE R GUEST

HOW TO PARTY CHIC

RENA KIRDAR

BE MY GUEST

HOW TO PARTY CHIC

ASSOULINE

CONTENTS

No Excuses:

Here are 10 reasons you should have a party!

1. It's somebody's birthday!

2. To combat the Anti-Social Movement:
We all spend way too much time online and don't get enough in real-life interaction. And that just isn't right. The best way to wage war on this phenomenon? A party!

3. To welcome a friend
or family member coming to town or to bid farewell to one who's leaving.

4. To kick off a season
or to celebrate a holiday: Christmas, Thanksgiving, Diwali, Easter, Cinco de Mayo, London Fashion Week ... everything is fair game.

5. Because you have a new set of plates you want to show off.

6. To set romance in motion.
Parties, especially dinner parties, are one of the best, low-pressure ways to set up a couple you think would be good together. Single? A party is the perfect excuse to see someone you fancy. Playing cupid at a party is how my dad met my mom: He saw her somewhere, found out his cousin was a friend of hers, and then made his cousin host a party so she could invite my mother!

7. For career purposes.
Parties can afford you and your guests with incredible networking opportunities in an environment that is enjoyable.

8. Because you're happy.

9. Because you're sad.

10. Because we all need to have more fun!

INTRODUCTION

A few years ago, my mother called, thoroughly distressed, because a woman she'd met went on and on about how she's heard all about me. Namely, all about how I throw the best parties. My mother disapproved. "What a shame—after all that hard work, degrees from Oxford and Columbia, and all people know you for is throwing a good party? How are you going to shake off this reputation?" Rather chastened, I hung up the phone wondering how indeed I would get rid of it. Then, a light bulb went off in my head. My reputation as a terrific party thrower was an asset I could use for something positive, productive, and fulfilling.

I often find the inspiration for my themes from books, and for a long time I had scoured the shelves for one that contained all the ingredients for a good party. There were plenty of books on table settings and décor, and lots of books on food and mixology. But there was no single book that covered the elements of a good party from A to Z. Nothing that documented the energy and verve of a party that had taken place. So, I decided to write one myself.

When I came to New York, I was introduced to Prosper Assouline, a man known for his vision and intuitive understanding of people. Within a few minutes of hearing me speak he said, "I love it, send me an email next week with the themes you plan to cover and how you execute them."

I pitched themes that I thought complemented the Assouline brand, but could be easily replicated by readers seeking inspiration for their own events. A Hot Hacienda for Christies to kick off their Latin American Art Sale, a Black, White, and Diamond gala for Chanel, The Jungle party for Roberto Cavalli, and a floral ball I titled *Scent of a Woman* to launch Oscar de la Renta's new fragrance were just a few of the parties that I organized and featured in my first book.

Two years after the initial meeting with Assouline and fourteen epic party themes later, *Be My Guest* was published. As for my mom, she has finally come to grips with the fact that the apple doesn't fall far from the tree. She herself is widely known for entertaining beautifully.

With this next book, I explore the unknown variable that takes any party and transforms it into a great party—what I call *R-factor*, or *Rena Factor*. R-factor elevates your party into a magical night you will remember for years. R-factor isn't about the food, amount of money spent, décor, or the venue. It's about creating a palpable energy you feel when you walk into an amazing party.

Is R-factor something that you solely stumble upon by chance, the stars somehow aligning on that one evening? Or is there some kind of formula to it? I would like to be so bold as to propose the latter. As with everything in life, of course there is an element of luck. There is a lot you can do amp up your R-factor and set the stage for hosting a night to remember. **And that's what *BeRguest* is all about.**

FOF: The Fear of Failure

I was once at a party and I saw a friend who's been reading my blog, *BeRguest*. He asked what to do about what he called the *FOF*. *The Fear of Failure*.

He continued to explain that while he wants to host a party, he's afraid of "failing." Concerned that people wouldn't have fun or enjoy themselves, that it would be a flop … and then what?

Here is my response:

1. The risk of having a party flop is greatly mitigated by going through all the elements of a party and sticking close to the guidelines recommended by yours truly.

2. The most important factor is the energy of the host—that means YOU! If you are having fun, that sets the mood for everyone else to have a good time. Guests will not have fun unless you are relaxed and enjoying yourself. Attitude is contagious.

3. Distance yourself from the emotional investment in the results. Do whatever you can, then let the chips fall as they will and disconnect a bit from the results. Stay Zen!

4. If the party doesn't work then you may need to ask yourself, "Do I have the right friends?" Some people, although lovely, just aren't good at parties. Have them over for tea or go out to the movies with them. Others are terrible and should just be consigned to the NIA List (p. 120)!

5. Remember that every host has failures. We learn from our mistakes; a failure or two are fine in the long run. You nailed something but flubbed something else? Take notes and move on. You'll get it right next time.

6. Keep your head up and your FOF will turn into CFS—an acronym I made up that stands for "Confidence for Success!"

For all the would-be hosts out there worrying about taking the plunge and throwing a party, feel the fear and do it anyway!

How to Throw A Party

THE ELEMENTS:
YOUR PARTY CHECKLIST

*Here's a handy checklist to make sure you have
all of your party elements covered:*

☐ The Theme
Whether it's a color scheme, an occasion, or a seasonal celebration, you've got to have a theme.

☐ The Guest List
• *How many*? Is this a small, intimate affair or are you going for a blowout bash?
• Who: the mix—making sure this is just not a bunch of friends hanging out who may as well be eating pizza. This is a party!

☐ The Venue
Are you hosting at your home or at a restaurant, or are you going all out and using a raw space?

☐ The Dress Code
Costumed, casual, cocktail, or black tie? You must clarify in the invitation.

☐ The Décor
• *Lounge areas:* if you have them, this is where your guests will mingle over drinks before dinner is served, and where they'll end up once dinner is done. Do not neglect decorating this area!
• *Dinner areas: a.k.a. the ever so crucial table décor.*
• *Centerpieces:* floral and/or otherwise. Get creative and use fillers!
• *Tableware:* plates, glasses, cutlery, obviously.
• *Linens:* napkins and tablecloths. You need these too!
• *Place cards* if it's a seated affair, which, if it's over eight people, it should be. People need to know where to sit!
• *Lighting:* Good lighting is key! We all need to look good, and it's a major mood creator.

☐ The Invitation
• *Digital vs. Physical:* how to create hype around your party.
• *RSVP's:* make sure you collect them.
And don't forget the day before/day of reminder!

☐ The Food

• *Pre-dinner nibbles:* You don't want your guests starving if dinner is running late.
• *Dinner:* Make sure the food is fine to eat, but it shouldn't be that good!
• *Dessert:* Always have something sweet on hand.
• *The midnight snack:* If your party is running late into the night, you should definitely have a midnight snack handy. Your guests will thank you for it!

☐ The Drinks

• *The cocktails:* Signature cocktails for a particular theme are nice. Also, I highly recommend my all-time favorite Spicy Margarita.
• *Your general bar:* Remember, cheap booze is a false economy! This is not where you should skimp!
• *Shots:* Want people up and dancing? Pass around trays of shots.
• *The dessert drink:* A nice touch but not absolutely a must.

☐ The Entertainment/ Music

• *DJ:* I would definitely hire one for bigger affairs.
• *Playlists:* It's all you need for your at-home dinner party.
• *Band/singer/entertainer:* I'm not so keen on live entertainment unless of course you just happening to be hiring Bruno Mars or Beyoncé!
• *Speeches:* If it's a landmark event, there will be speeches! I think speeches are always nice to make the occasion more memorable and special, even if it is just a small dinner.

☐ The Seating

• Who sits with whom: so important!
• And who sits where is somewhat less important in my book.

THE GUEST LIST:

It's all in the mix. Why your guest list should be eclectic.

Having secured RSVPs from the ideal mixture of the Big Five (p. 19), you might think you have on your hands an incongruous group that won't gel. Instead of the familiar crowd that knows each other inside and out, you've got people from different walks of life with seemingly nothing in common. If you feel that way when you look at your guest list, i.e., out of your comfort zone, well done! That's your first step towards hosting what is guaranteed to be an unforgettable evening and possibly the best party you've hosted to date!

Comfort zones

If you're feeling apprehensive, it's understandable. Mixing up crowds like this may not go over so well with some of your friends (Type 1 of the Big 5), especially if they tend to be a cliquey, insular group.

Why is the mix so pivotal?

Going through the effort of hosting a dinner party, or getting dressed up and going to a dinner party, makes me excited for some new energy, and at most to walk away with a new friend or acquaintance who will hopefully enrich my life in some way.

The mix is where the energy of the evening springs from. For your guests, it's much more interesting to see different faces, meet new people, and have different conversations than the ones they would normally have. Making sure the mix works is where you as a host get to work your magic. And by magic, I mean strategically mapping out your seating plan ... don't be afraid. Mix it up!

THE BIG FIVE:

The five guests you need to invite
to make your party the mother of all parties!

I may not be the best person to advise on this topic, since I always want to invite everybody to every party—other than those who have made it onto the NIA (p. 120) list. My parties are notorious for being the tightest squeeze ever with some people going so far as to actually grumble about it, my husband included.

Having said that, here is my two cents on who you should have on your guest list to make your party the best party it can be!

The Big Five:

1. Your friends: This may sound obvious, but what I mean is that at the top of your list should be your close friends. The ones you call and spend time with informally, no occasion necessary.

2. People you like but don't know so well: It is so nice to be invited to something that you didn't expect to be invited to. You get to meet different people, possibly make new social connections, and get to know your host better. A party is the perfect opportunity for you to reach out to acquaintances like these and truly expand your social circle.

3. A professional connection, whether actual or potential: An informal gathering on your turf is by far the best way to explore or nurture a professional connection, whether it's for yourself or a friend you're fond of. A new job opportunity, a promising business venture, a valuable mentoring relationship—any one of these can be on the table.

4. A love connection, whether actual or potential: Dinner parties are a great setting to foster a love connection, whether it's for yourself or a friend. Throwing a set-up into the mix also adds a bit of intrigue to the evening for the other guests. In my book, that speculation on how "it" is going is always a welcomed addition at a dinner party and adds to the ratings of the evening.

5. The wild card: The interesting/fabulous/(in)famous guest that you may not know so well, but who you can somehow get to attend your party. That's guaranteed to add that little bit of sparkle and possibly some unpredictability to the evening.

ON INVITATIONS:
THE PARTY STARTS HERE

Invitations should be intriguing.

A good invitation will get guests to start thinking about the party as soon as they receive it. A good invitation will guarantee they'll want to attend, and if they can't make it, simply receiving the invite should elicit a major case of FOMO.

As much as I love a physical invitation with flourish, I'll be the first to admit that I've fallen victim to the digital age. I love and have come to depend on the convenience and organization afforded by the e-vite.

E-vites are my new BFF since they make things incredibly easy. My online account has all of my various party lists with all my contacts, and reminds me of all the rude people who haven't RSVP'd on time to do so, and sends reminders to my guests the day before the event.

But while it may be easy, affordable, and good for the environment, sometimes an e-vite—even in our digital era—just doesn't cut it.

Invitations for big occasions, like weddings, elicits physical invitations—usually in the guise of a beautiful and sturdy oversized card.

Another instance where I feel going beyond the e-vite is a must is when I really, really, really want my guests to get psyched for my event, like a themed costume party. I start off with an e-vite to find out who's coming, then follow up with something special. For example, a hand-delivered package containing a mask for a masquerade ball lets my guests know that I mean business!

Recently, after the RSVPs come in, I've gone very digital and began using video montages with images and words to suggest what guests should wear. It's unambiguous and means that my party props won't get lost in the courier mail shuffle.

In the end, it's important to understand that the invitation is more than just a means to deliver the what, when, and where. It's the medium through which the mood is conveyed to my guests, and a way to jumpstart the party by getting my guests to show up in the right frame of mind.

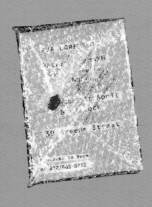

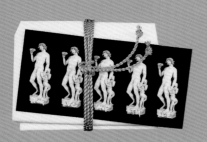

ON PLUS ONES
(AND TWOS)

The answer is usually 'no thanks'

While seating affords wonderful opportunities to orchestrate an evening, it can be tricky to pull off due to last minute cancellations. What's worse than that? The guest who brings along uninvited guests in his or her wake ...

The Date

In most cases when the person I've invited is dating someone, I already know about it. Which means that I would have already invited the 'couple'. If my guest is in a fledgling relationship that seems like it's going somewhere, I'm happy to host my friend with their plus one—so long as I'm prepared for it.

However, when guests ask if they can bring a random "date" along at short notice, I begin fuming. Not to mention that as "uninvited" by me, those dates do not reciprocate thanks for the hospitality, because we are not properly acquainted.

I'm all about coming up with a seating plan that maximizes the odds of a well-choreographed evening. I'm only able to do that to the extent that I know my cast of characters. Throw one unknown into my mix and my careful planning has gone out the window.

The exception

Sometimes, just sometimes mind you, the date is amusing, interesting or has star quality that makes them Wild Card material that can add an element of unpredictability and fun to the night. When the plus one falls into that category, the date-bringer is usually quick to share this with me and eager for me to want to have them.

The houseguest

If I'm hosting a dinner party and I want to invite sixteen people, it means I could actually have about twenty-five to thirty guests.

In instances when the person requesting has offered me good hospitality or is a close friend, I grin and bear it. Especially when these house guests are great additions. If they are not, I simply apologize and explain there is limited seating space but that their guests are welcome to come afterward for drinks. If they can't leave their house guests behind, then everyone can drop by for drinks afterwards. Not that I don't love my guests, but not everyone works in every situation.

The bottom line is that asking your host if you can bring along more guests than you've accounted for, it is always difficult. As guests, we must respect our hosts and not expect that it's okay to start making up their guest lists for them!

ON DRINKS:

Tips for getting your guests tipsy

Your house is immaculate, your dinner table is dazzling, the lighting is perfect, your play list is on point, and you've invited the right mix of people—including your Big Five. Technically everything is on the right track for a fun-filled evening packed with R-factor. But let's cheat a little ... A bit of booze certainly can grease the wheels of a party.

What kind?

I'm a sucker for signature cocktails. And I like coming up with signature drinks that fit with the theme that's in play. Wine, of course, should be served, but in a party of over thirty people, I would not serve red wine. The risk of spills is too high!

How much?

There is *nothing* worse than running out of drinks midway through a party. It's better to have booze left over than to run out.

Serving it up

For larger parties, I am a big believer in shots. They're easy to drink, gulp-sized, and help get people in the mood. Upon arrival, hand your guests a shot and make drinking it compulsory for them to enter the room (unless they don't drink). Hard liquor shots can be hard on the stomach, so I recommend shots that are mini versions of sweet cocktails. Trays of shots should be plentiful throughout the night. It's important that people have full access to drinks, so I end up putting bottles on the table so guests can help themselves and not have to wait to be served. I also like to set up a bar for guests to go up to even if there are servers at the party.

The Liquor Cabinet

While I am a big believer and proponent of cheap and cheerful alternatives so as not to break the bank when entertaining, the quality of alcohol would not be where I skimp. I don't want my guests blaming me for their terrible hangover or making snide remarks about the booze in the post mortem. Also, many of your guests may not be drinkers, or not drinking that night for whatever reason, so it's always important to have non-alcoholic options. If you're doing signature cocktails, a non-alcoholic version of that should be on hand.

Keep the buzz going!

Whether at home or in a restaurant, people often have tea or coffee to close the meal and wind down. However, sometimes I rather naughtily replace the tea with Long Island iced teas and the coffee with espresso martinis!

ON ENTERTAINMENT AND MUSIC

Don't let the entertainment get in the way of having fun

If you're having a party, you should have some form of "entertainment" or music. For a small dinner party at home, all you need is a solid play list. For bigger parties where you want people up and dancing, go with a DJ.

When we become an audience, energy levels plummet. This is why so many people nod off in front of the TV, pass out at the movies, or start snoring at a play. But no one falls asleep while gyrating on the dance floor! A good party is defined by one thing only: The energy. I don't care who performs, who caters dinner, or whatever else is going on, if the energy, or R-factor, aren't right, the party is a flop and waste of money and effort.

But, I get it. For really big special occasions, weddings and benefits, we always feel like a DJ just isn't enough—we have to do more! Analogously this happens to me when I'm going to a major function and I feel like getting my hair done at a salon despite knowing that I do it better myself. When it comes to hiring a band, it is really very difficult to get it right. If the band is bad, it kills the party, and no one wants to dance. If they're good, it becomes a show, and the energy levels drop. It's a lose-lose situation. If I absolutely must hire a band, I make sure that they aren't just good musicians, but good performers.

Hiring a bongo player, a saxophonist, or a violinist to play alongside the DJ is also a great way to ramp up the music while still having the songs we know and love sung by the original artists themselves. The key is to find a performer who will augment the energy rather than work against it.

Finding a good DJ is key, and it is not at all about how expensive the DJ is. In fact, the opposite is often true, since more 'important' DJs will play whatever they like or think is best, while less 'fancy' DJs are more likely to take requests, heed your directions when it comes to what kind of music you want to hear, and pay attention to the play list you give them. The bottom line is that no one is coming to your party to see a concert or watch a show. Your guests are there to mingle and dance. And the best way to get that to happen is to hire a good DJ.

Apart from a DJ, the one kind of entertainment I like to hire are those that help beef up the theme for costumed parties. Dancers that perform for a *very* short time, such as belly dancers for an Arabian Nights theme or Carnival dancers for a Brazilian party.

ON SEATING

Placement and the importance thereof

Dinner parties should always be seated, with placement, unless they are buffet-style. Seating placements are both the best and worst part of throwing a dinner party. When you nail it, the party is sure to be a hit; and when you get it wrong it's a killer.

Surprisingly, many hosts have no clue about seating, including people you would think have it down, given how frequently they entertain! Others are under the false impression that seated affairs are boring and stuffy. Seating, when done properly, is the way to make the night *fun!*

What makes seating so important?

Clever seating is how you get the party going, whether it's fostering animated conversations or getting guests dancing. It is part of the magic that puts people in the best mood and ready for having an amazing time!

The good news is that anyone can up their seating game and take their dinner party to the next level. It just requires time and thought while keeping a few useful pointers in mind.

Etiquette, configuration & spatial awareness.

I've now stressed the importance of seating placements. It takes the longest time and requires the utmost precision—just one minor change can alter the entire social landscape. Now it's time to talk about how to get it right!

There is a protocol!
The seats next to the host are the seats of honor. The seat to the right of the host is superior to that to the left. As a rule, I set these seats aside for high priority guests. These are:

a. The guest being feted
b. The older guest
c. The guest who I don't know very well, or I have invited for the first time
d. The guest of professional importance to myself or my husband
e. The best friends
f. The guest from out of town or who has travelled a distance to be there

Sometimes, when certain guests are in some way difficult to seat or would be considered a 'bad' seat, I take one for the team and seat them by me.

Configuration matters.

Round tables are somewhat easier to seat for than long and narrow tables. However, my main concern with a round table is who the two guests sitting on either side of Guest X will be. With long and narrow tables, the dynamics between six guests need to work: the two next to Guest X and three opposite him or her. And with long narrow tables, I always seat guests at the heads, otherwise the poor guest at the end of the table is sitting alone and it becomes a dead zone.

When there is more than one table:
> **a.** I do not put all the most 'important,' or most desirable guests at one table, nor the 'not-so-important.'
> **b.** I try not to create 'ghettos' of the same nationality, industry, or background. Everyone from all walks of life should be mixing!
> **c.** I try to give the 'weaker' tables better placement in the room, and 'better' tables a lesser placement.

Your table is a chessboard.

When I work out my seating plans, I draw out the table and mark how many seats there are. This paper is then put into a transparent plastic folder. I write out the names of my guests on sticky tabs (with different colors for the men and the women) and that way I can move them around and envision how the tables will work.

Don't start too early.

One cancellation throws the whole plan off, so you may as well not start this challenging undertaking only to have to chuck it out and go back to the drawing board. I never work on my seating plan until the very last minute, because there are always last-minute cancels. For a big party, I start working on my seating chart a few days before, but if the crowd is under forty, I do it the day of.

Mixing and Matching.

Eventually you can hone your mixing and matching into an art of your very own. Until you do, here are my tips on how to get there.

Break 'em up!

I never put couples together unless they are a very new couple or if someone is bringing a date as opposed to their actual significant other. Otherwise splitting couples is a must.

If I want to spend the evening talking to my husband, why would I want to be at a dinner party when we could be doing exactly that from the comfort of our home? When couples are seated together, they make less effort to speak to those around them. It deflates the dinner conversation dynamic and dims energy of the table. Breaking up couples during the meal helps post-dinner circulation. There is the natural inclination to seek out your partner afterward, which creates good flow—and flow is key!

Mix 'em up!

It is *boring* to seat friends or people who see each other on a regular basis together. You want your guests to enjoy their companions at the table. It's all about devising a thoughtful mix, so I take time thinking about who would like whom and *why*. This means potential romantic or professional connections—people I could see liking each other and becoming friends, have an interesting dinner conversation, or create a fun dynamic that would enhance the whole evening. These may not be overt at first glance, so taking the time to think what an interesting but not-so-obvious connection could be key.

Do the unexpected.

When hosts work out placement, they're usually hyper-cautious and resort to putting like next to like. They'll cluster people by profession or income and bunch younger guests at a kiddie table and elderly guests at an oldie table.

I love going to a dinner party and finding myself seated next to someone I would never ordinarily meet or speak to. Don't be afraid to seat a sportsman next to an artist, mix the downtown crowd with uptown, or place a banker beside a manufacturer. However, be on the safe side. A rule of thumb is to seat a guest next to someone new on one side and someone with whom they're more familiar on the other side.

The one exception:
I love mixing, but one thing is for sure—if you have an intention of getting guests on the dance floor, you need to put the fun people together and cordon them off from the bores. People think that you need to distribute the fun people, but that is one-hundred percent wrong. Seat a fun person next to a dud and the dud kills the vibe.

How to Attend
A Party

HOW TO GET OVER FOMO: FEAR OF MISSING OUT

Making sure it doesn't ruin your day, night, or life!

If you were Not Invited:

1. Read 'How to get invited to every party' (p. 38) so you are always invited in the future.

2. Post fake party pictures on social media so people assume you had a prior and more exciting engagement.

3. Convince yourself that you never wanted to be at this party anyway so you're grateful not to have been invited to begin with.

4. Shelve your various social media addictions and instead spend that time doing something you enjoy. Book a spa appointment; binge on your favorite television show; read a good book; or hang out with someone you love.

5. Plan your own fabulous revenge party and invite everyone but the person that didn't invite you.

If you were invited, but couldn't make it:

1. Realize that everyone at the party is obviously not having any fun whatsoever without you—you're the life of the party!

2. Turn off all social media.

3. It is incredibly bad taste to cancel on an event because a 'better offer' came along. Make sure everyone knows you were in fact invited by posting remarks on social media afterward in the vein of "I wish I could have been there..."

4. Focus on what it is that you are currently doing and realize that it is much more valuable than attending that supposedly fabulous party.

If you were invited, but didn't particularly want to go:

1. Realize that if you really don't want to go, you most likely will be miserable, emanate bad vibes, want to leave early, and as a result, be a bad guest. Guests like that end up on NIA lists. Remember that it's much worse to not get invited at all than get the invite and choose not to go.

2. Recall the principles of The Big Five. If you're going just to avoid FOMO and don't particularly like the host, then how are you going to be able to reciprocate the invitation?

3. Remind yourself that you probably aren't missing out on anything life changing.

HOW TO GET INVITED
TO EVERY PARTY

What's better than throwing a party? Going to one! You don't have to plan, cook, or clean up afterward—just get dolled up and enjoy yourself. Here's how you can add to your popularity, boost your social life, and make sure you never experience FOMO again!

☐ *1.* Throw parties and invite people. Despite just talking about how much nicer it is to be a guest rather than a host. This is at the top of the list because it is the best way to get invited. If you host people (and do a good job of it), nine times out of ten they will invite you to theirs.

☐ *2.* Study the NIA list carefully and make sure you don't fit into any of the offender categories.

☐ *3.* Don't pigeonhole yourself into one set of friends: While it's great to have a consolidated group of pals, cliques are limiting. Make an effort to expand your social circle to develop friendships with different groups of people—you'll always have a party to go to.

☐ *4.* Become the life of the party so people fall under the impression that their do would flop without you.

☐ *5.* Make sure that you fit the bill for at least one of the BIG FIVE types for everyone you know. However, while ticking one of the BIG FIVE boxes that may get you a first invitation, it won't guarantee a second. A host appreciates a guest's enthusiasm, both pre-, during-, and post-party. Make sure to convey that enthusiasm when you receive the invitation, RSVP on time, and stick to your commitment. If you absolutely need to cancel, then make sure you have a valid reason and that you have done so well in advance. Be an engaged guest during the party and do not leave early. And always make sure to thank your host after the event.

SAVE THE DATE!

Because my party is definitely more important than that other party

Ideally invitations should go out weeks in advance; for a destination parties, MONTHS in advance. But what's the word on 'Save the Dates?' Should we even bother with them? If so, then when should a Save the Date go out? What format should it be in? How much info should a Save the Date contain? Here are my thoughts on the matter:

Situations that Require a Save the Date:

When you're contending with other people's big events—especially their weddings: Summer is wedding season. Despite sending out my Save the Date nine months in advance, I already had a few people let me know they won't be able to make it because they have weddings to attend that same weekend.

Couples plan their weddings sometimes two years in advance and pin down their guests early! If you're planning a big party, never mind a wedding, letting people know sooner rather than later with a Save the Date means you can secure guests whose calendars are still open before they get flooded with other invitations—usually for weddings.

When you're asking your guests to travel to celebrate with you: When it comes to destination parties that involve out-of-town travel for your guests, a Save the Date well in advance is a MUST. With booking flights and hotels, giving your guests the chance to be that early bird who plans to get the best available options at the best prices is just common courtesy. Traveling to go to a party is already somewhat of an indulgence and a luxury, having time on their side to secure the best options at better prices is something your guests would appreciate very much.

How to do it

Keep the info general: When you send out a Save the Date, chances are you don't have all the details worked out yet.
While a proper invitation should reflect the theme of the party, a Save the Date doesn't need to do that. Don't let the pressure of having every detail in place delay you from hitting the send button.

The medium: You can send a Save the Date by email, snail mail, or most conveniently, via Paperless Post.

The Cons:

1. It doesn't carry the same weight as an invitation,so it's not a fail-safe way to determine who's coming or not.

2. You raise your guests' expectations super early on, so if you don't deliver they'll be disappointed.

3. Both you and your guests may get bored of the whole subject of your party by the time it rolls around. This happens a lot with weddings.

4. You get too many enthused yeses when you know the space at the venue you really, *really* want is limited.

5. You can't change your mind about having the party or changing the date. I mean, you can, if you want to, but it would be a bit embarrassing/confusing. People would probably understand, but still ….

6. You can't change your mind on the guest list. What if someone lands him or herself on your NIA list by the time your party rolls around, but they already got the Save the Date?

7. What if you meet new people you want to add on in time for them to attend, but there just isn't enough space, and now you're stuck with the guests that are already on there but just aren't as appealing anymore?

PARTY-GOING PROTOCOL: THE 'THANK YOU'

(And why it's an absolute must)

This is by no means a 101 on etiquette. In fact, I'm hoping that most people reading this are wondering why on earth anyone would have to write about something so basic as saying 'thank you.'

A shocking number of people don't say thanks after you've had them over. It's a basic principle found across almost every culture and religion: treat others how you yourself would like to be treated. People who entertain recognize this and so, duly thank their hosts after attending a party. People who don't entertain, however, may not recognize the value of saying 'thanks for having me.'

The handwritten thank-you note

Nothing is more divine than the receipt of the handwritten note (and preferably hand delivered, so that your host gets it the following day). Ideally the note would contain copious references to details from the night before—the more the better. It shows your host that their efforts were noticed and appreciated.

The electronic thank-you note

That is, the text or email message. I must admit that I'm guilty of often choosing this option over its admirable handwritten counterpart for the sake of convenience. If the message is the same and includes plenty of details about the night before, this form of thank-you is perfectly acceptable. It's also the bare minimum.

The thank-you flowers/confectionary

For a regular dinner party, if the host isn't a close friend or it's the first time you go to their home, it's good practice to either take something along or send it the next day. If you opt for flowers, my advice is not to send them on the day of or before the event unless you know that person's home décor or the floral scheme they've set up. Otherwise, your flowers might clash. If your host is a very close friend or someone who hosts you regularly, a gift or flowers is not a must … a note, call, text, or email will do.

The thank-you gift

Birthdays are a mandatory call for gifts. Even if your host says 'no gifts' on their invitation, it's nice to bring something along. It doesn't have to be an expensive gift, just thoughtful. I love anything personalized. It shows effort was put into it. Scented candles or picture frames may sound generic and boring, but they are great gifts because one can never have enough picture frames, and candles always run out. Wedding gifts are also mandatory—thank God for gift registries!

The bottom line is, you should send a thank you—whether you call, write, or send something, even if it is just a few minutes to acknowledge the effort that your host made for you.

Party Themes

DINNER IN THE LIBRARY

Sensory Overload in a Good Way! Maison Assouline's Cabinet de Curiosités: a dinner party venue like no other …

I will be the first to admit that I've thrown parties before simply because I've wanted to show off a new set of plates that I was extremely proud of. When my dear friends Prosper and Martine Assouline opened up their flagship London luxury cultural concept store in the autumn of 2014, Maison Assouline, I naturally wanted to show it off! Two years later I finally got the chance to do exactly that when Prosper invited me to host, as an ambassador of the brand, a very special intimate dinner to celebrate the magnificent space they had created. As such, this was one of those rare instances when the venue was the theme as well. Here's why:

The Theme and The Venue: Assouline's Cabinet de Curiosités

Maison Assouline occupies an iconic building on the bustling Piccadilly Street, steps away from the Royal Academy of Arts and, for the tea lovers out there, Fortnum & Mason. The building, designed in 1922 by renowned British architect Sir Edwin Lutyens, once housed the prestigious Hauser and Wirth Gallery, making it a most befitting location for what the Assoulines have transformed into a rarefied haven for lovers of books, culture, and the finer things in life.

The main floor sells books, accessories, gifts, candles, and other chic objet d'art. It is also home to their Swans Bar, which serves food and drinks throughout the day. The true jewel of the venue lies two floors up in an extraordinary library room known as the Cabinet de Curiosités. The room's ceilings soar at 3.5 meters, and its original pre-WWI wood paneling and moldings are kept pristine. If the room itself isn't enough to impress, the collection of furniture (both contemporary and antique), vintage books and objets, art, sculptures, carpets, and everything else is enough to cause major sensory overdrive. The best way to describe it would be to imagine if the Palace of Versailles had a love child with Aladdin's Cave of Wonders—It is an absolutely jaw-dropping space.

The grandeur and old-world glamour of the room, coupled with a desire to emphasize just how special the event was meant to be hosting a more intimate affair. Although the Cabinet de Curiousités could accommodate many guests comfortably, I restricted myself to just twenty guests.

To be perfectly honest, I find smaller dinners far more challenging to organize because the body count is crucial. Every single guest counts and all the individuals must click. Carefully look through all the permutations because, even with a seated affair, the pre- and post- dinner drinks and mingling mean a natural flow is of prime importance.

A group of people who were already friends with each other would be too dull, so I wanted a group who for the most part didn't know each other, but who would have things in common and would want to get to know each other. Of course, it had to be a group of individuals who would be interested in Maison Assouline as a concept store built around culture with the taste level to truly appreciate the magnificence of the setting.

I structured my guest list to reflect the spirit of Maison Assouline, bringing together people from the art world, fashion, restaurant, and film industries.

The Décor

In a room filled with objets, my challenge was to showcase the merchandise as much as possible while creating a non-commercial atmosphere. Luckily, the merchandise happened to be almost everything in the room, all of which were unique and gorgeous items, so it wasn't that difficult of a task.

We rented tables that could be put together to create a surface wide enough to accommodate the abundance of items I wanted to use, and long enough to fit twenty guests. I covered it with a chocolate brown linen tablecloth to serve as the canvas for the epic dinner table arrangement I was going to create. Everything I could find that wasn't pinned down went on the table: a set of 1950s brass drums, a Bengal leopard skin, a genuine Samurai helmet circa the 1820s, Ernest Hemingway's Louis Vuitton trunk from the 1930s, several leather bound volumes of *Egypt Explained* dating from the 19th century, and an 18th century snake trumpet that was used to play baroque music in its time. To cap things off, four beautiful and unique René Gruau chairs from the 1950s headed the table on either end. Every element of the décor was a conversation piece, and Prosper was on hand to answer questions the guests had about the objets.

Rob Van Helden, one of London's most talented florists, breathed life into all of this gorgeous antiquity with spectacular floral arrangements that complemented the library atmosphere of the Cabinet de Curiousités. The result was visually stunning and certainly stimulating. I lavished the table with pomegranates, a fruit that to me symbolizes ancient world opulence. I found some beautiful thick wired red and gold ribbon to tie the napkins with, and attached red and burgundy faux flowers onto them.

The Space

I wanted to divide this awe-inspiring and somewhat imposing room into a living area and a dining area to create a homey feeling and to facilitate the flow of the evening. An afternoon of moving around furniture with Assouline's wonderful Eugenio, maître d' of the Swans Bar, and his team resulted in something I was quite proud of. We managed to create a few intimate corners for guests to gravitate to for one-on-one conversations.

MENU

Fillet of Salmon Tolstoy

Terrine de Foie Gras, lightly toasted Pain Brioche

—

Spinach & ricotta ravioli served with Alba truffles

—

Atlantic steamed cod Mediterranean style

—

Maison Assouline bitter chocolate ice cream

Bûche de Noël - Panettone with vanilla sauce

—

Coffee & Petit Fours

Wines

Chablis Domaine Colbois 2014

Château La Croix Chantecaille
Saint Emillion Grand Cru 2011

Food The menu was equally indulgent and special, adding to the delight of all our senses. We started with slabs of sumptuous smoked salmon and rich foie gras courtesy of the Swans Bar, followed by a melt-in-your mouth ravioli topped with freshly grated truffles, flanked by a buttery steamed cod. Dessert was a bitter chocolate ice cream and bouche de Noël for dessert—a seasonal winter menu fit for kings.

The Music A mix of upbeat Latin music with Afro-Caribbean roots. Since this was a smaller gathering, we kept the volume low so the conversation could flow.

The Energy All our senses were beyond stimulated on all levels—absolutely scintillating. Just looking at the set-up alongside the Assouline team had me beside myself with excitement, and I was thrilled when Prosper and our guests said they felt the same way. Most of the guests had never been to Maison Assouline before, much less having set foot in the concept store's amazing Cabinet de Curiosités.

Given the lavish setting, delicious food, and a carefully thought out guest list, the R-factor was off the charts. Everyone left the dinner party on a high, telling me they couldn't remember an evening that they had enjoyed as much. Each guest had met at least one new person who they planned on seeing again—one of the biggest markers of a successful dinner party.

The formula

A space that feels like study or a library—dark wooden paneling is a bonus

•

Interesting objects from around the house that one wouldn't necessarily think belonged on the dinner table—just stick them on there and go with it

•

An interesting and eclectic group of people

•

Autumnal bouquet with leaves

•

Rich reds and browns— think branches and red roses, but go beyond that

•

Pomegranates. Lots of them

5 Game-changing Party Décor Hacks

☐ 1. Start with a theme and a color palette

A theme party can be something as simple as a color scheme. Focusing on a theme, especially when it comes to coordinating colors, makes it easier to tackle the task of decorating.

☐ 2. Spray paint

Once you have your theme and your color scheme, finding things in those hues may not be so easy. You can spray paint just about anything: branches, fruit and vegetables, flowers, vases, potpourri—the list goes on! If you need to repurpose a prop for another party theme, you can always spray paint it another color.

☐ 3. Add some sparkle

To make the most of your lighting, get with the glitter: glitter spray, glitter confetti in glass containers, and loose rhinestones. Glitter plus candles equals maximum pizzazz with minimum effort.

☐ 4. Make your flowers fuss-free

If you're no Ikebana expert, don't fret about flowers. Bouquets are passé, so there's no need to hire a florist. You can still achieve a striking effect by sticking to one color or kind of flower and DIY. I bunch my flowers tight and low into my vases—after spray painting them if the theme calls for it.

☐ 5. Keep candy handy

Strewing small bowlfuls of candy and chocolate wrapped in your theme colors is the oldest trick in the book. Not only do these bonbons reinforce your theme choice—you give your guests with a sweet tooth something to nosh on.

NO SHADES OF GREY

A black and white Christmas

The idea of a non-traditional Christmas theme is something unique in the sea of red, green, and gold that dominates the aesthetics of the holiday season. I boldly decided that black and white could indeed be made to look Christmassy and festive, all the while channeling Truman Capote's legendary Black & White Ball. It's also an easy theme to ask people to dress for, as everyone has black or white in their closet.

The Living Area

Our living area is divided into two sections, one that is more neutral with black, white, and gold accents, and the other in turquoise, which we proudly refer to as our Peacock Room.

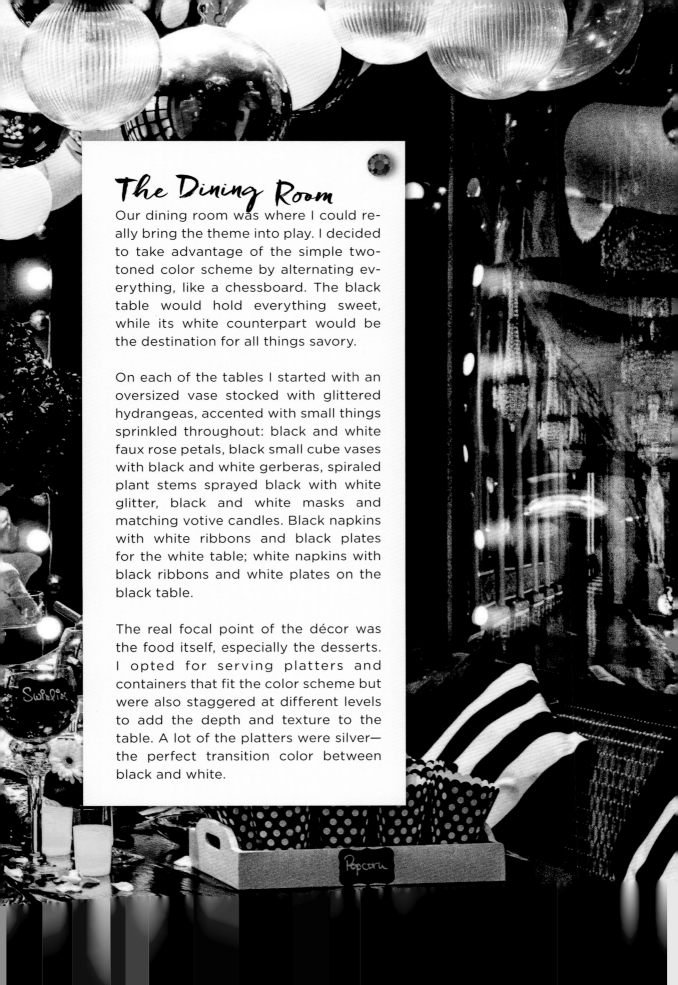

The Dining Room

Our dining room was where I could really bring the theme into play. I decided to take advantage of the simple two-toned color scheme by alternating everything, like a chessboard. The black table would hold everything sweet, while its white counterpart would be the destination for all things savory.

On each of the tables I started with an oversized vase stocked with glittered hydrangeas, accented with small things sprinkled throughout: black and white faux rose petals, black small cube vases with black and white gerberas, spiraled plant stems sprayed black with white glitter, black and white masks and matching votive candles. Black napkins with white ribbons and black plates for the white table; white napkins with black ribbons and white plates on the black table.

The real focal point of the décor was the food itself, especially the desserts. I opted for serving platters and containers that fit the color scheme but were also staggered at different levels to add the depth and texture to the table. A lot of the platters were silver—the perfect transition color between black and white.

The Guest List

The guest list was massive—we wanted to host everyone we wanted to celebrate with before going off to have their own more private Christmas celebrations.

The Venue & Format

Every year, my husband and I host our annual Christmas party at our home, for which the theme changes but the format remains the same. It's what I refer to as an open-house buffet dinner, with music and dancing as well as more low-key mingling. Our party format gives people the option to stop by anytime throughout the evening.

The Décor

I had never been more excited to decorate a Christmas tree! I stuck on all the things that I had frantically ordered from Amazon over the past few weeks ... black and white feather boas, black and white masks, black and white lollipops, large white butterflies, black and white lights and oversized light-up gift boxes. Once all of these special items were on the tree, I filled in the rest with black and white baubles. The result was unconventional and yet completely Christmassy. I did the same with the wreath on our front door, adorning it with the black and white lollipops, black and white ribbons and black and white battery operated bauble lights. This year, our garland was bedecked in black and white ribbons, black and white feather boas, and the aforementioned black and white swirled lollipops.

The Food

The open-house buffet dinner is all about not having a fixed dinner time. Having finger food available all night means guests can eat whenever they are hungry. Although I'm all about dinner parties, I believe that the food involved should always be easy and reliable. We had eleven different items that catered to both carnivores and herbivores alike.

The Entertainment

While I love playing with my décor, food and music are elements of a party that I tend to be a bit less experimental about.

The Drinks

Alongside the usual beverages, we served iconic black and white cocktails—espresso martinis, eggnog, White Russians, Black Russians and Patron coffee shots.

The Sweets

This was the true crux of the décor for the party, so I went all out. I created a dessert bar on a black table with all different kinds of candy jars and stands. All the candies and desserts were black and white; jellybeans, licorice, marshmallows, Oreos, chocolate mousse, black and white cupcakes, oversized white meringues, swirled black and white lollipops, and black and white popcorn boxes filled with sweet and salty popcorn.

100 people in total came, half who stayed for most of the evening, while the rest filtered in and out. This made it feel like we were having multiple parties throughout one night. Around midnight a surprise guest—a major movie celebrity—popped in having been invited by some of our close friends. His entrance just catapulted the energy into another dimension. Everyone was super excited that Mr. X was there, so the R-factor level exploded.

The combination of the excitement over our surprise guest, alongside the music, the wild décor, and that infectious feel-good Christmas spirit made for such an amazing evening that I spent the following day wishing I could rewind to the night before!

The formula

B&W masks

•

B&W lit balls

•

B&W glitter branches

•

B&W candy
jellybeans and swirled lollipops
are key here, but anything you
can get your hands on in copious
quantities works

•

Different sizes and shapes of
candy jars and cake stands

•

Faux B&W rose petals

•

B&W feather boas

•

B&W baubles

•

B&W gerberas

•

B&W glittered hydrangeas

•

Poinsettias and other plants
generously spray-painted in
black and white with heaps of
glitter on them

•

B&W votive candles

•

B&W napkins wrapped in black
and white ribbon for napkin rings

•

Black stickers and white chalk
pens for signage

•

B&W paper candy bags

•

Budget-friendly Ikea black and
white bowls and B&W cushions

•

B&W everything, basically

LOTP:
The Life of the Party

There are some people who just make the party. They attract people like a magnet with their contagious energy—the ones who always look like they're having a blast, tend to be a bit louder than the rest, and always have a crowd of people hovering around them. Basically, "the cool kids."

Quiz! Are you an LOTP?

1. **When you receive an invitation do you**
   a. Check that it was addressed to you and not sent to you by mistake.
   b. Know that you're clearly a last-minute filler since the event is three hours from now.
   c. Check your exploding diary.
   d. Throw it in the bin.

2. **At the party do you**
   a. Pretend to be texting on your phone so no one will try to speak to you.
   b. Stay glued to one person all night.
   c. Find a strategic position where you can hold court knowing the party will come to you.
   d. Do nothing but eat.

3. **The day after a party do you**
   a. Think that last night was a waste of time.
   b. Not remember a thing.
   c. Have aching feet, seem to have lost your voice, but otherwise feel like you're on top of the world.
   d. Wake up and go to 9am yoga because you went to bed at a reasonable hour the night before.

If you've answered mostly C's, congrats! You just may be an LOTP!

Being the LOTP

I always say I carry the party in my handbag. Metaphorically—I usually carry clutches to parties. But that means that I make the best out of any situation and have fun wherever I go. And I think that qualifies me as the LOTP.

How do I do this? Well, I'm so glad you asked!

All it takes is...

1. **A positive and optimistic perception of people:** I always look for and try to bring out the best side in people because I believe everyone has something beautiful to offer. That means that I'm engaged with whomever I happen to be talking to. Theoretically, that makes any conversation I have more interesting and fun. Unless that person is trying hard to be unpleasant.

2. **Being open and being able laugh at yourself:** I am very open and like sharing things about myself (provided these things aren't completely inappropriate). This happens to be a great icebreaker. It attracts people and immediately puts them at ease. And not taking myself too seriously is a huge component of that icebreaking quality.

3. **It's all about the mood I go out in:** As in the mood I leave the house in. If I don't feel good, don't think I look good, or think that I'm not going to have fun, then I am guaranteed to have a terrible time. It is mind over matter. Think it, project it, act it, feel it. Everyone has problems, but a fresh happy person at the table is the one people gravitate to. And good energy is contagious!
Speaking to that, we have ...

4. **Music:** the great mood manipulator. I put music on at home while I'm getting ready before a party to get me in the mood to be the most vivacious version of myself. And I'm known to get involved with the music situation at the party too, either by handing the host my party play list or asking the DJ for songs that I love and that I know for sure will get the party rocking.

Inviting the LOTP

Even though I consider myself a LOTP in my own right, as a host I really want an LOTP at my party. That's because the LOTP is usually who gets the dancing started, makes sure that no one is bored, and picks up any of the social slack for me as a host in case I'm overwhelmed by everything that goes into hosting. The right LOTP can turn out to be the Party MVP.

1. **Secure the LOTP:** Of course, the LOTP is a very popular guest to have, so I make sure to give them plenty of notice! They need to be the first to know that I'm going to have a party.

2. **Seating the LOTP:** If it's a seated affair I *never* make the mistake of putting the LOTP next to a bunch of wet blankets—who really shouldn't be there to begin with! While he or she will be able to converse with everyone and anyone, the best way to make sure the LOTP is in top form and adding to the energy and R-factor of the party is to put them around people that will feed the fun.

3. **Make sure you want the LOTP:** Many LOTPs are personalities that can at times be overwhelming. They can sometimes dominate the dinner conversation, and the party then becomes the [insert name of LOTP here] Show. There are situations when that's a good thing, but others when it really isn't.
Which brings us to ...

4. **How many LOTPs to have at your party:** I like to have at least one LOTP at a party to feed the fun. My rule of thumb is one LOTP per every 10 guests. Any more and one may have a clash of LOTPs (not good), any fewer and the LOTP will be stretched too thin, leaving some guests feeling like they're being left out of the fun.

A SENTIMENTAL AUTUMNAL AFFAIR

Two themes, one great party

Landmark birthdays are a big deal and, in my opinion, *must* be celebrated with flair. When my father turned eighty—a huge occasion for any family—we wanted to throw him an epic birthday party. My mother, sister, and I planned for a year prior. We decided to host an intimate affair at our family home in Cap D'antibes, asking our guests to spend the weekend with us in the South of France. The main event, a black-tie party at our villa that Saturday night, was split into two parts: a lavish dinner, followed by an after party.

The theme(s) Two things defined the theme of the evening: the time of year and the man of the hour. Fall is a beautiful time in the South of France, and we wanted to use all the hues of the season—rich reds, deep yellows, oranges, and greens.

Focusing the theme on my dad, we decided to use as many photographs for various aspects of the party. My sister, Serra, and I spent hours poring over all of the old family photo albums, picking out the pictures that represented the most meaningful moments for my dad and our family. A lot of them were in black and white, so that color scheme came into play a little later in the evening.

The Guest List Because this was a destination party in an intimate setting, we invited only family and my parents' oldest and closest friends. The final head count ended up being around eighty people—the perfect number for an 80th birthday!

The Décor After cocktails in the living room, we escorted our guests to a transparent marquee we set up in the garden. It featured chandeliers covered with flowers, twigs, leaves, and crawling vines. Centred on one side of the marquee was a large screen that projected a slideshow of all the photographs we had chosen throughout the evening. Leaves, miniature pumpkins, orange wedges, and chestnuts were artfully scattered on the tables and used to form autumnal bouquets. Glass vases, clay containers, and multi-level copper candelabras completed the table spread. As an additional touch, we sprinkled the tables with personalized M&Ms, with photos of my dad on one side and his initials on the other.

Table Names and Signage With seating, it's always fun to come up with clever alternatives that correlate with the theme instead of table numbers. My dad is very proud of having published four books, so we decided to name our tables Chapters 1 through 8, with each chapter representing a decade of his life. We had talented artist Linda Fabrizius draw caricatures that reflected the significant events and achievements that marked each decade. These were framed and placed on each table as signs. We had the caricatures printed onto the menu covers as well.

The After Party

After dinner, the revelry moved to another marquee that had been set up as a lounge and dance floor area. The tent's ceiling was canvased with fairy lights, and the space was furnished with minimalist white leather lounge seating. The lounge sofas were strewn with cushions, both sides of which featured a collage of the black and white photos we had selected. We rolled out the cake at this point in the evening, a large four-tiered affair encased in white fondant and frescoed with black and white photos from the past eighty years.

The Entertainment

Because we split the evening in two parts, we distributed the entertainment throughout. During dinner, the fabulous Sami Goz performed with his band.

During dinner, we included three truly personal elements in the entertainment. First, my sister, our three children, and I all got up to deliver a short speech to my dad. Next came a video montage made by my father's longtime assistant, Sharon. Some of my father's closest friends screened a short film they had made together, which was sentimental.

At the after party, we surprised my father with a performance by one of his all-time favorite singers, Ilham Elmadfai. An Iraqi musician of international renown, Ilham's music evokes wonderful childhood memories for my father, who grew up in Kirkuk, Iraq.

The speeches, videos, and the photographs evoked a lot of emotions. The degree of warmth and the outpouring of love that filled the room was something that even I, as a seasoned party thrower and goer, had never experienced before.

We had set out to plan a sincere and unique tribute to a wonderful man who has left his mark on the world in so many ways.

The formula

Sunflowers

•

Mini Pumpkins

•

Orange Wedges

•

Autumnal bouquet
with leaves

•

Chestnuts

•

Personalized orange
and green M&Ms

•

Caricature table signs
and menu covers

•

Copper candelabras

•

Personalized photo cushions

Let them eat cake

Or maybe just look at it …

Birthday and celebration cakes used to be functional. They were basic in terms of presentation—just your standard layer or sheet cake iced in traditional buttercream and tagged with messages like 'Happy Birthday Sandra!' or 'Congratulations!' scrawled in royal icing. What was on the inside was what really mattered. If you were serving a good, proper cake, it had to be delicious and moist, and the flavor had to be one of universal appeal. These days, cake is no longer just a cake. It's an elaborate production that focuses on the story the cake tells. As these cakes become more like sculptures and less like baked goods, I raise the question: Does anyone still eat cake at these parties anymore?

Even though I think these crazy mega cakes are beyond fab, people should not feel obliged to have this served, even as a presentation. A cake that tells a story doesn't necessarily have to be so complicated. Pivoting off one thing that's idiosyncratic to the person being feted is enough. Is the birthday girl a gym rat? Layer cake decorated with gym gear does the trick. Even with simpler cakes, guests can still be hesitant to dig in. If you want people to have some cake but still make it special, cake pops and cupcakes are good alternatives. No messy slicing involved, they're easy to eat, and your guests can practice portion control if they're so inclined. There's also the bonus of being able to mix and match now that bakeries are concocting creative new flavors.

If you go all out with your cake, spending a ton of money to depict an epic saga, it may just have to be a feast for the eyes and not the tummy, but it'll be a nice memory to look back on years later.

EMMA'S BAT MITZVAH

Jenny Symonds and Emma's Fairytale Fantasy

My close friends Jenny and Geoff Symonds recently celebrated the Bat Mitzvah of their daughter, Emma. Jenny, a professional party organizer herself, whom I've known since 1991, is one of my most creative and talented friends. It's not surprising that she took her daughter's Bat Mitzvah to a whole other level!

The theme(s) Jenny's main objective was creating a Disney's Cinderella Ball atmosphere. Her daughter was symbolically transitioning from a child to adult, so she wanted to indulge in the childhood fantasies a girl might have. It was a youthful and magical environment that worked well for both the younger and older generations in attendance.

The Invitation Jenny believed the invitation set the tone for the event and made her guests excited to attend. She sent out a physical invitation that was more personal, with embellishments like a personalized stamp and confetti make it much more exciting.

$\mathcal{E}$

American Entree

Roasted tomato soup, truffle aranchini, basil oil

British Mains

Ladies:
Pan fried fillet of cod, bubble & squeak potato cake with crushed peas, asparagus,
heirloom tomato and lemon verbena sauce

Gentlemen:
Braised beef short ribs and slow cooked rib eye with braised onions, roasted root
vegetables, coriander mash potatoes and red wine braising jus

Australian Desserts

Pavlova, meringue, vanilla whipped cream and exotic fruits
OR
Hedgehog melting sphere, chocolate biscuit, caramel sauce and vanilla ice cream

Wines

White - Chablis Ier Cru "Montmains" Simonel Febvre 2014
Red - Chateau Haut Beausejour 2012

14 January 2017

The Décor

Jenny opted for a color scheme of turquoise blue and silver—Emma's favorite color—to lend the room that Cinderella magic. On one side of the ballroom two long tables of forty-eight people each were set up for Emma and her friends. The kids' tables were accessorized with paper lanterns, light-up letters spelling out E.M.M.A, and jars of blue candy. For that magic dust feeling Jenny used sequined tablecloths and covered the ceilings in oversized confetti balloons that had party hats and pompoms dangling off them.

The other side had sixteen tables of ten for the adults. Oversized fake roses ringed with fairy lights in glass display domes channeled Disney's Beauty and the Beast.

A huge believer in party favors, Jenny had strewn acrylic boxes filled with silver chocolate balls topped with either a koala bear, Big Ben, or the Statue of Liberty, spray-painted silver across the tables. An additional room was stocked with personalized goodies for the kids. Jenny set up a photo booth and Instagram square for a fun guest take-away memories.

The Food

In keeping with the multi-cultural theme, Jenny had an American starter, a British main, and an Australian dessert. In addition to a picturesque American candy bar, an ice cream bar, a crêpe stand, old-fashioned popcorn machines, and trays heaped with chocolate chip cookies rounded out the after-dinner treats.

The Guest List

Despite having 260 guests, because each one of them meant so much to Emma it still felt like an intimate gathering. How intimate a party feels is not about the number of invitees, but about the quality of their relationship to the host.

The Venue

Jenny originally didn't want to host the party at a hotel, but The Savoy turned out to be the place that ticked most of the boxes—both in terms of logistics and ambience.

The Entertainment

Jenny, Geoff, and Emma's two older brothers delivered heartfelt speeches. Jenny's present to Emma was a video montage that included interviews with all the people closest to Emma. Not wanting to leave anything to chance, Jenny gave the DJ a list with pages and pages of songs.

A surprise for the girl of honor was a special performance by 19-year-old Matt Terry, who had just won X-Factor. The kids went wild when he came out.

Emma and her family had an amazing time, and when that happens, it's contagious. The little touches Jenny put the effort into and the amazing music made this party a feast for the senses. 110 out of the 260 guests had flown in especially for the occasion, so there was a very special, warm family feeling to the party.

Répondez
s'il vous plaît!

Why you should RSVP. And be quick about it

When I get an invite, I check my calendar. If I'm free and I know I want to go, I immediately RSVP 'yes,' same for 'no.'
So why can't everyone else get their RSVP act together?

Are they:

a. Waiting for a better offer? Are these delinquent RSVPs hesitant to commit because they expect another event's invitation is coming their way? I would rather the holdouts decline my invitation from the get-go.

b. Afraid of seeming desperate? To those insecure people who think RSVP'ing right away comes off as desperate, my answer is au contraire! The busiest people with the most active social calendars are usually the ones who respond the fastest because they want to nail down their commitments.

c. They just can't be bothered? It boils down to being either inconsiderate or totally oblivious. If it's the former, they belong on the NIA List. If they are the latter, it may be because they never entertain themselves and so they may not understand why it is imperative to RSVP promptly.

Why is this RSVP business so important?

1. **The numbers:** No matter how big or small the party is, capacity is always limited. If someone can't make it, I need to know ASAP to invite someone else before it's too late.

2. **The little touches:** To plan a great party, I need to know who exactly will be coming. This doesn't just impact seating, it also throws a wrench in planning out things like personalized gifts and place cards to arrange for well in advance. These small, special touches make all the difference.

3. **The attitude (of gratitude):** Part of being a guest that hosts want to entertain repetitively starts before you arrive to the party. RSVP'ing promptly shows appreciation. And as a host, it feels nice to invite people who are flattered to be invited and look forward to attending.

There are some exceptions, however...

1. Parties abroad: The only invitations where you should take your time RSVP'ing are the ones that involve travel. However, most destination party invites are issued well in advance with 'RSVP by' dates clocking in at least several weeks if not months before the event.

2. Justifiable concerns: If you are holding back because of a dilemma, like unconfirmed travel plans or family commitments that you aren't sure of, PLEASE communicate them.

ANGELS & DEMONS PARTY

I rolled out this fantastic theme for a client's 40th birthday. What was great about this event was that I had the opportunity to go all out and create two separate spaces— double the creativity and double the fun!

My client's property was perfect for this theme. They had a large garden where we set up a marquee as our 'Heaven' for the first portion of the evening, which was a dinner. For the second half of the evening, we ushered the guests into a hot-red 'Hell' nightclub.

Heaven With the help of superstar florist Rob Van Helden, we created a Garden of Eden. Ghost chairs flanked white tables that were topped with a lush green moss. The centerpieces were branches that were either ornamented or topped with baby's breath that resembled fluffy clouds. Concealed within these clusters we placed one red apple here and there for guests to find. And soft yellow lighting was used to create heavenly light beams, clinching the look.

Hell The space was long and rectangular so it lent itself easily to being converted to a lounge/nightclub area. We set up banquettes with low lounge tables in black and red on opposite sides of the room. I had a red neon sign made inviting guests to get rowdy and 'unleash their demons'. I ordered this one online—there several companies that do this beautifully. Finally, red sconce lanterns cast an infernal effect again, lighting was key here!

Tips Alternating place settings on just one table, or having some tables marked as heavens and ones as hells, are all ways to make this theme work. Even better, you could designate one room in your home as Paradise and another as Inferno. Then declare your foyer, hallway, or whatever as No Man's Land in between these two rooms as Purgatory.

This theme is especially marvelous because of its dress code. Unlike other full-on costumed themes, people are more than happy to accent their outfits with cherubic or impish flourishes. If you want to do a dress-up theme that is easier for your guests to get into, go for Angels & Demons. I guarantee that some beautiful wings (both leathery and feathery), halos, horns, tails, and harps will be on show!

How to create a veRy Rena dinner table

And why getting creative with your dining table will generate R-factor

Entertaining at home can be hard work, but it's by far my favorite way to host, mostly attributed to setting up my dinner table: I love seeing my friends' awestruck expressions when they make their way to my dining room. Major R-factor points! A beautiful dinner table isn't just for the talented or for the wealthy that can afford to hire the talented. Arranging the table for your own dinner party can be a fun, creative, spontaneous, and an incredibly rewarding process. My dinner table is how I express myself to the family and friends that sit around it. And you should do the same as well! Over the years, I've hosted dozens upon dozens of dinner parties at my own home, so I've finessed the art of setting up my jaw-dropping dinner tables into a eight-step process.

Step 1: Brainstorm the theme

Every party I throw has a theme that ties it together. Deciding my theme can be influenced by the season, occasion, or something I saw in a coffee table book. I think about the theme for a few days and use Pinterest to create a mood board.

Step 2: Select a backdrop

Once I've fixed on my theme, I move on to finding the tablecloth—the canvas! If I don't find anything that works with what I have in mind, I head down to a fabric store and buy a few yards of the perfect cloth for the theme.

Step 3: Take inventory

I see what things I already have and can use for the theme. This helps keep my budget in check because I never buy something I already own. I rescue any items that could work from the garage, give them a good cleaning, and set them aside for later.

Step 4: The sundries excursion

I head down to the flower market in the early morning a day or two before my dinner party to scout for fresh flowers and other sundries that I can use with what I already have. Apart from my general theme and color scheme, I usually don't have much in mind about what I intend to create. After one loop around the market, I formulate ideas about what I want and go back and buy the things I like. While it's always a good idea to set a budget before you go, the wonderful thing about the flower market is that the vendors are wholesalers. You will always get more bang for your buck there! I use the term "sundries" because the flower market doesn't just sell fresh flowers, it sells every decorative item imaginable. Glittery branches in every color, decorative seasonal dried fruits, feathers, shells, vases, candles, ribbon, raffia, and more! I like using non-florals for table centerpiece creations: masks, fruits and vegetables, candy, and any other decorative knick-knack from around the house that happen to work with the theme. I often use these elements as my base and then accent around them with flowers rather than the other way around.

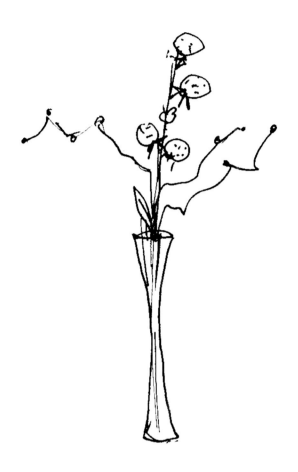

Step 5: Do the flowers

Cutting, cleaning, and arranging the flowers is by far the most difficult part of the process. And yet, rather than hire someone, I always do it myself. The DIY dinner table can be embedded with personality and originality that no third party can ever deliver, no matter how professional. Don't be afraid to do your own flowers! I keep my bouquets tight and bunched up, no stalks showing and the greenery completely trimmed off. I dislike having one token arrangement, so if I'm going with six roses per vase, I would usually have anywhere from six to twelve of those arrangements on my dining table.

Step 6: Bring it all together

With everything prepped and cleaned, I get all my partyware and flowers on my kitchen table behind me for easy access—that's when the real fun begins. I get to play with the various ingredients that I now have ready and see how things work together. There is A LOT of trial and error involved. I often wind up using things in ways I had never thought of before. Often, items I bought but went unused are brought out from the garage and get repurposed for a new theme years after the party they were originally intended for.

Step 7: Set the table

I like using different items for place cards according to my theme. I've written made ID tag bracelets that doubled as both napkin rings and place cards, and engraved wine glasses with guests' names on them. Ribbons or raffia are my go-to for napkin rings. One thing I don't play around with: my napkins are always white. I collect plates and have all colors and brands. But with so much going on in the center of the table, I prefer using more neutral plates. I tend to rely more heavily on my Crate and Barrel plates than my fancy patterned chinaware. With respect to glassware, when it gets a bit rowdy the last thing you want is to worry about your expensive Baccarat glasses. Save your crystal for when your great aunt comes to visit.

Step 8: Step back and admire your handiwork

This is my favorite part of the process because it always surprises me. The next time a similar theme or color scheme comes around, even if I use some or even all the same ingredients, the result is always completely different.

Creating a beautiful table for a dinner party at home shouldn't be a matter of breaking out your finest silverware and sticking a bunch of flowers in a vase. An elegant dinner table is not about adhering to a generic rulebook. Entertaining at home and creating your own dinner table arrangement is an occasion for all of us to express ourselves, to have fun, and to open ourselves up to others. THAT is the definition of warmth and hospitality—two of the key components of R-factor. A beautiful DIY dinner table that you've put thought and effort into adds a little extra something to a party that will make the evening all that more special.

WELCOME TO TOWN

Dennis & Michael

I'm always thrilled to see my New Yorkers when they drop by London. Luckily two such friends are NYC-based fashion designer Dennis Basso and his husband Michael Cominotto. Since they're here so often, Dennis and Michael have become close to many of our friends in London who look forward to seeing the couple when they are in town. Last they were, I invited a group of friends they already knew along with some they didn't, but who I thought they might enjoy meeting.

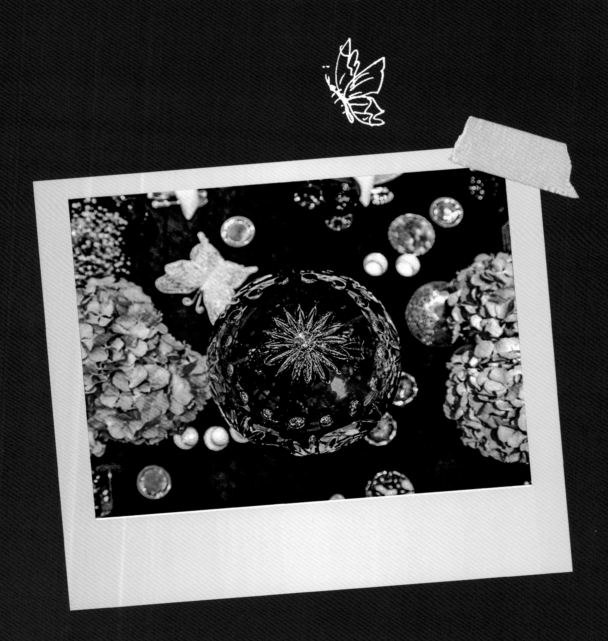

The Guest List I limited the group to a mere twenty-two guests so we could comfortably fit around the table.

The Décor For the table décor, I took a trip to the flower market, where I immediately fell in love with mauve hydrangeas one of my favorite flowers, and although expensive, when in season they have such big heads that you don't need that many to create an impact. To add some textural variety to the table I also picked up some pink baby's breath.

The pink hue got me enthused for spring, and I got excited about mixing it with the cobalt colors of my dining room. Bringing home my flower market purchases, I settled on a pink, purple, cobalt, and white color palette.

I located my blue tablecloth, white candelabras, white butterflies, a sprinkling of faux diamonds, white and silver chargers and plates, and cobalt blue votive candles. For place cards, I ordered individual personalized meringues from Meringue Girls that came in clear plastic boxes. Pink meringues for the ladies and blue meringues for the gents, and a few extras in the event of having to call in a last-minute alternate or two!

The Food

I like to stick to what I know works when it comes to food—we had our usual Lebanese fare. But for dessert, I decided to be a bit more adventurous. I called up Lola's Cupcakes and ordered individual cheesecakes in a variety of flavors, including salted caramel, blueberry, chocolate brownie, cookies and cream, and banoffee pie.

The Energy

A little welcome toast to Dennis and Michael was in order to remind everyone why we were here, introduce our friendship to those who didn't know them as well, and celebrate having them here in London with us!

The formula

Friends from out of town

•

A nice mix of guests

•

Our very own dining chairs

•

Hydrangeas in pink and blue

•

Pink Baby's Breath

•

A blue table cloth

•

White candelabras

•

Cobalt blue votive candles

•

A smattering of faux diamonds

•

White and silver plateware

•

White butterflies

•

Color-coordinated candies

•

Meringues as place cards

•

Blue and purple twine

•

Lebanese catering

•

Adventurous desserts

My NIA list

The seven kinds of people I never want to invite again!

Every morning after I throw a party, my husband watches in bemusement while I get out my 'Never Invite Again' list, making additions to it. It may seem harsh, but my preferred type of entertaining are seated affairs. This means that I spend hours on the placement, putting in a great deal of thought into where each and every guest is seated. For every party there are so many people that I would have liked to invite but did not have the space for. **My 'NIA' list is composed of:**

1) The Last-Minute Canceler:

Nothing infuriates me more than getting that eight p.m. message, 'Sorry, I can't make it tonight, I'm sick ...' It's too late to even begin to change around the table, so the offender has created an empty seat. Unless they're in the ER, last minute flaking is unacceptable. The ones who cancel (even well in advance) for a 'better offer' are actually the worst of the lot! Thanks to social media, these utterly gauche social deplorables get caught out in their lies sooner rather than later. Personally, once I commit I never cancel, no matter how appealing another option might be. You either decline or try to make it to drinks afterward.

2) The No-Show:

Not having the courtesy to inform the host you won't be coming is rude!

3) The Placement Changer:

Even if I'm hosting 300 people, I know exactly where each person is seated, and, like a hawk, I notice right away if someone has changed the seating. Each seat has been carefully selected and, in my book, it's a huge social no-no to change the way the host has arranged it.

4) The Guest who has not Adhered to the Theme or Dress Code:

If someone has no intention of complying with the dress code requested by a host, they should decline the invitation. If they've accepted, they have to make at least a minimal effort to get dressed up. Guests who don't comply with the dress code can make the ones who have feel uncomfortable. Also, they just ruin the look of the party.

5) The Guest who looks Miserable and Leaves Early for No Reason:

Accepting a dinner party invite is about a lot more than just happening to be available that night and being up for a free meal. If someone doesn't feel well or motivated to socialize, they should decline an invitation. Guests need to come ready, looking and acting the part. It's not a question of being the life of the party, simply making the effort to try and enjoy themselves is enough for me.

6)The Non-Reciprocator:

Of course, I understand that I entertain a lot more than most people. That's because it's what I love to do. But every time I make up a guest list for my next dinner party (which is pretty much at the same time as I update my NIA list), I stumble upon people that I realize haven't invited me to anything in forever. In fact, the only times I do see them is when I'm the one doing the inviting! Otherwise I never even hear from them. While they may not be hosting lavish parties to invite me to (a lot of people find entertaining stressful), they should at least reciprocate by asking me to something – the movies, catching up over a cup of tea, even a glass of water! The idea is that they have the interest and want to make the effort to see me in whatever format they're most comfortable with. I don't think that's too much to ask.

7)The Ones Never to be Heard from Again:

After having made the effort to host and entertain guests, whether it's a grand affair or a more casual get together, it's polite to hear from your guests the next day. Thank-you notes, gifts, and flowers are amazing, but the fun post-mortem phone call is my favorite. Party follow-up communicates that the effort that went into the party didn't go unnoticed or unappreciated. I award bonus points for people who still send hand-written thank-you notes—it's a slice of old-world etiquette that's so thoughtful and yet seldom seen. But even a text, whatsapp, or email will do the trick.

THE JUNGLE PARTY

A walk on the wild side

The Jungle theme draws out the wild side of everyone—attending lets them explore their animal nature, whether they want to channel a sexy python, a virile tiger, or an impish monkey. It's the perfect theme for when you'd like your guests to let go of their inhibitions and have a wild time! Calling all wild things, I invited my guests to come celebrate my birthday dressed as 'predator or prey.'

The Invitation I sent out an invitation that only hinted at a jungle theme, asking guests to RSVP in order to receive the details. I then sent out an email to those attending letting them know that it was a Jungle Party with 'predator or prey' dress code. I attached a short video to give my guests costume inspiration, letting them know I wanted them to push the limits—they were welcome to go as wild as they wanted.

The Guest List As always, the Big Five, this time 150 of them. It was a squash to say the least. But that was very much in keeping with the theme ... it was a zoo!

The Venue I needed a venue that was going to be cool with an evening that was going to be anything but tame. Luckily, a friend of mine introduced me to restaurant owners who were prepared for the wilderness that we were importing for the night.

The Décor My goal was to turn the restaurant space, which had modern wooden interiors, into a tropical rainforest. That meant lots of lush greenery and tropical flowers, animal prints galore, tribal masks, and toy animals. Eleven tables were covered in as many different animal print fabrics we could find, and "trees" crafted from branches, palm leaves, and tropical flowers were planted in clay pots as centerpieces. A few votive candles rounded it out.

Table Names & Signage

I went with fun animal names like "Hip Hippos," "Za Za Zebra," "Eye of the Tiger," "Monkeying Around," "The Lion King," and "Elephant in the Room." The fabulous Edward Bowie made rustic wooden signs that had the names and a related drawing next to them. These were slung low from the ceilings over the tables they represented. I used matching plastic and stuffed animals as the mascots for each table.

In lieu of the usual escort cards, guests received a key ring with miniature animals and the name of their tables. Of all the preparations that I have ever undertaken for a party, this was by far the most tedious and complicated, and impossible to delegate or get help on. Every time I switched someone's seat around, I had to remember to not just change the tag with the table name, but to change the animal too! I like to think that the effort entailed in getting small details like these right are appreciated by guests and in turn they make the effort to get into the spirit of the party. Extras included using broad tropical leaves as the place cards. Guests' names were written in gold marker and the leaves were attached with an animal print clothes peg to the raffia tied to the napkins with.

The Parrot

The Food

This was one of those situations where the food was not the focal point of the evening.

The Drinks

With minimal food eaten and plenty of drinks consumed, this party transformed into a jungle very quickly! For the signature cocktails, I requested that they make tropical-style rum-based cocktails such as Mai Tais and Piña Coladas served in coconuts and pineapples.

The Entertainment

From the beginning of the night I had the fabulous Ozzy, a talented bongo player drum alongside our loyal DJ Adnan, creating a rhythmic sound that enhanced the jungle vibe the minute guests walked in. On its own or alongside music, the bongos are a fantastic party atmosphere-booster.

Two of our dear friends gifted me with two surprise acts. The first was the original Tight Fit, the pop group that covered The Lion Sleeps Tonight in the 1980s. Tight Fit was followed by a brilliant Elton John impersonator who, of course, played music from Disney's *The Lion King*. He did such an amazing job that the next day some of my guests were telling others, with true conviction, that Elton John had performed at my party!

This theme is incredibly easy to pull off from a dress code point of view since even your most straitlaced female guest has at least one animal print item in her wardrobe, and it's easy for men to get their hands on something appropriate as well. And it can be taken as far as one feels comfortable while still including the more fainthearted in a mere leopard print dress.

Trust me—once you throw one jungle party, you'll find yourself itching to throw another one sooner or later.

The Energy My guests, many of whom are buttoned-down in their day-to-day lives, looked and acted the part of untamed creatures. There was dancing on the tables, swinging from the vines—they all went a bit mad and any inhibitions they might have had were cast off!

It was certainly a night to remember. People made a huge effort with their costumes, coming in full on animal garb with unrecognizably painted faces and leaves, and clad in very little actual clothing in some instances! We had Zulu warriors, a giraffe, a variety of primates, and just about every other wild animal you can imagine.

The formula

'Trees' made from branches, palm leaves, and tropical flowers

•

Tablecloths in different animal prints

•

Animal print clothes pegs

•

Rustic wooden table signs

•

Tons of plastic and stuffed animals

•

Mini plastic animals tied to key rings with raffia for escort cards

•

Raffia and monstera leaves for the backs of the chairs

•

Monkey nuts

•

Ozzy the bongo drummer

•

DJ Adnan

Friend Poaching

Major faux pas.

Friend poaching happens when one person introduces a friend to a third party, and when the two hit it off, and in the end exclude the person who originally brought them together.

For a while I thought my visceral reaction to friend poaching was just possessiveness. Then, I started getting questions about this exact topic from the nicest people. With validation on a subject that I thought I was alone on, I decided friend poaching merits further examination. If you came to a dinner or event and clicked with someone you'd like to see again, that's great! It means that as a host, the job has been well done, and that is exactly what socializing is all about. But there are rules:

1. Thank your host

Let your host know they did a nice job with the mix, compliment them on their great taste in people, and thank them for how thoughtful they were to have introduced you to the new wonderful person in your life.

2. Share the love

The first get-together with the new acquaintance, whether it's lunch, drinks, or a party, needs to include the host who made the introduction. This is common courtesy. **Exception: A first romantic date. The host need not chaperone.**

3. Acknowledge the point of origination

Basic fact of life: people meet through others. There are times when we want to meet certain people that we know are friends of friends. For work, fun, friendship etc. I often ask my friends to make introductions for me and am often the recipient of introductions. At some point the new acquaintance you made at your host's party may develop into a closer friendship than the one you share with your host. However, a measure of respect needs to be shown to the originator of the introduction.

4. Don't be a pouncer

These are folks who shamelessly pounce on your most "desirable" friends—whether they're rich, famous, gorgeous, or simply fabulous. Nobody likes to admit that we are friends with pouncers, much less admit that we might be pouncers ourselves. They might camouflage well, but when in the company of people who somehow fit the above 'desirable' criteria, the beast emerges and the pouncer can't help themselves. Some people dismiss it saying, "pouncers are gonna pounce." However, it turns me off and I've had to call people out on it at my own parties!

THE POP STAR
KARAOKE PARTY

A walk on the wild side

he **Theme** My sister Serra *adores* karaoke. For her birthd
 my living home into a full-blown karaoke bar. I sent out an in
 friends to get ready to sing their hearts out and come dressed
 stars!

The Guest List

A themed costume party means a massive guest list. But because Serra is very particular about who she likes to spend her time with, she wanted to limit the group to about thirty-five guests. Her guests have been her friends forever, and so they all came ready—and dressed up—for a fun night to celebrate their dear friend.

The Décor

It was inspired by Serra herself as well as by the pop star theme. Serra's favorite color is electric blue. Luckily, my dining room is that shade of blue, so I didn't have to do battle my already existing décor!

I found the perfect backdrop for my table spread—a black tablecloth with an electric blue rose print. I added some drama to the table with stark white candelabras. Blue roses, feather boas, and bowls of blue confections filled in the gaps. I also bought about twenty toy glitter microphones from Amazon that I made into arrangements in vases. My daughter and I and Serra's nine-year-old son wrote sweet birthday messages on a few small chalkboards dotted across the table. On the buffet table, I placed five oversized silver letter balloons that spelled out 'SERRA.' Lastly, I hired blue portable uplights for the floor, creating a nightclub atmosphere that was brilliant.

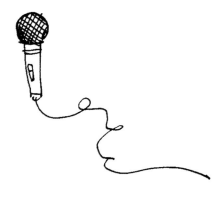

The Energy Everyone was in insane outfits, belting out our all-time favorite hits from Madonna, The Eagles, ABBA, Michael Jackson, and Britney. It got everyone going and created an interactive environment in which everyone bonded

The Food

The dinner was a homemade buffet. We had a mixture of some Lebanese cooking and mezze graciously supplied by our parents' household, as well as a big bowl of pesto pasta and a giant salad that we had made at home. I kept dessert simple with an S-shaped chocolate birthday cake, berries and two cake stands filled with Ben's Cookies.

The Drinks

Everything was available, but my Spicy 'Ritas made a special appearance. We also passed around caramel vodka shots after dinner as part of dessert.

The Entertainment

The entertainment was simply an at-home karaoke system that we rented. It came complete with a massive screen; all the controls; thousands of songs; revolving party lights; speakers, and four microphones. They delivered it on the afternoon of the party and came back to pick it up the next morning. It was ridiculously easy and was a massive hit!

The formula

Close friends

•

Pop Star costumes and people
willing to get into them

•

A crazy karaoke setup

•

Lighting

•

Everything electric blue and
pop star-ish that I could find

FLOWER POWER

I love my birthday! I really do. And usually, I celebrate it with a full-on costumed theme party like my Jungle Party and the Glam Punk party I threw. With this theme, I decided to cool it with my own birthday and have just a girls' luncheon instead.
As a rule, 'lunch' is not my favorite party time-slot but this time it just really felt right. And of course, when I say, 'just a girls' luncheon,' it wasn't just any old luncheon!

The theme(s) Since it was a birthday lunch in late June, I themed the event around flowers and bright colors.
Floral prints were much in vogue, so I thought this would be a great theme, not only in terms of décor, but that one my girlfriends would really enjoy dressing up for it.

The Venue

The most important ingredient for this party was the venue. I really wanted an outdoor event but needed to have a sheltered space—it may be summer, but we were in London after all. So, when I decided that I would take the year off from my big themed bashes, I called The Ivy Chelsea Gardens and booked their gorgeous greenhouse. Because The Ivy is subject to neighborhood noise restrictions, hosting an outdoor event in that coveted space could only be done during the day. And that's how I ended up with a floral-themed luncheon ...

The Invitation

My next port of call was Paperless Post to choose an invitation that would set the tone for the event I wanted to create. Luckily, I found just the perfect one. Florals with bright colors—exactly how I envisioned the décor.

The Guest List

When it came to putting together the guest list for this birthday, there were so many more people that I wanted to invite but couldn't. The Ivy was only comfortable hosting a party of up to forty people at a time, and I was already going to be way over capacity. Luckily, I entertain frequently enough that I can make up for it by inviting different people to different things.

RENA'S BIRTHDAY 22 JUNE 2017

The Drinks

I had some options. Green juice—in the spirit of keeping things healthy(ish). And, of course, everything soft, in addition to Bloody Marys, Champagne, and rosé.

The Day Of

After an intense heat wave, the forecast for the 22nd of June was all thunderstorms and showers. I was panicked, to say the least. I mean, this was London, we all expect it to rain ...just not on our parade, or our floral luncheon, as the case may be. But somehow, the stars aligned and the weather was perfect—cool enough to wear the denim jackets that I had made, but warm and sunny enough to make for a beautiful day.

The Energy

Even though this was 'just a girls' lunch' I had a blast. It was unapologetically girly and gorgeous!

The Extras

Other than the birthday girl, the venue, and the tablecloths, it was the little extras made this party stand out .... First, instead of place cards, I made personalized denim jackets for each of my guests. Typically, I came up with the idea very late in the game, so the hardest part was scouring the Internet to find a supplier that just happened to have forty-plus denim jackets in an assortment of sizes ready to ship. After miraculously finding a supplier, I had the jackets shipped directly to artist Jo Weir (who did the walls for the Glam Punk party) letting her know that the theme was florals and bright colors. I also asked one of my *BeRguest* illustrators, Marta Halama, to make an illustration that included every single one of my guests. So, I had to provide her with the guest list and a link to photos of each of my friends ... An arduous task but so worth it! Each invitee took one home as a keepsake. The last extra were these multicolored flower garland headbands that I had bought at the market in St Tropez. I used those as napkin rings but of course, we all couldn't wait to put them on!

MAK'S 46TH BIRTHDAY

*Not the smoothest dinner party I've thrown,
but even I mess up sometimes!*

Birthdays are the best reason to celebrate a person. For the 46th birthday of my husband, Mak, I set out to create a table that reflected him. This was incredibly easy because my husband is a fun-loving Lebanese banker whose favorite things include vodka, cigars, and me!

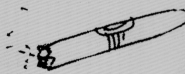

This was an intimate dinner for thirty of Mak's favorite people. Birthdays, particularly smaller affairs like this one (for us, thirty is small!) aren't so much about the Big Five as about who that person's real friends are. Still, the dining room was crammed elbow-to-elbow—typical of the Abbouds.

 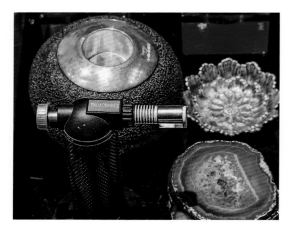

The Décor I went for a black, gold, and electric blue color scheme. Black and gold are very masculine but glam—the glam factor reflecting his choice of wife! The blue was an expedient choice to ensure that things matched my dining room.

I used a black tablecloth as my canvas and topped my long table with items that were "very Mak." Cigars; a bronze smoking bust; palm leaves sprayed gold, and two oversized gold vases that resembled vodka bottles. My plan was to use these idiosyncratic objects as the main décor elements, then accent all around them with flowers. Black vases housed fresh blue roses as well as roses sprayed gold; the vodka vases were stocked with the black glitter hydrangeas I recycled from our Black & White Christmas party.

NB: Glitter hydrangeas last forever. Literally. I have some gold ones in my room that I have had for four years! I would advise anyone throwing a party to invest in these because you'll get years of use out of them.

Speaking of recycling, I rolled out the 'Mak' signage, posters, and cushions that I had made for last years' party—I am a firm believer in cutting waste by reusing items from previous parties. But it comes at the price of a garage fit to burst with party décor.

Other table props included a copious amount of faux gold coins and jumbo calculators (because not only is he a banker, he's this family's accountant!) and bottles of Grey Goose vodka (his favorite) in a huge bucket of ice. I picked up some fun extras like the mini glitter top hats to top my napkin rings, and black and gold straws from the cheap and cheerful Tiger. I also ordered paper lanterns and ornaments from Amazon in my color scheme that I would play around with on the table. An extra special touch were the place cards, tied to jumbo nougat cigars, that my talented friend and Host with the Most Jenny Symonds designed for the occasion.

Lastly, I ordered six large clear balloons stuffed with black, gold, and cobalt blue confetti and a giant gold 'M' balloon from Bonbon Balloons to round out the décor.

The Food

Our usual, super-reliable and delicious Lebanese! I ordered a red velvet cake in the shape of a giant cigar, which was apparently a less reliable choice; although I had none myself, I was told the cake was a bit on the dry side.

The Drinks

Lots of Grey Goose vodka. I had the bottles set up nearby Mak because he likes to play bartender. And, because some things must stay consistent, my favorite Spicy Margaritas were also in circulation.

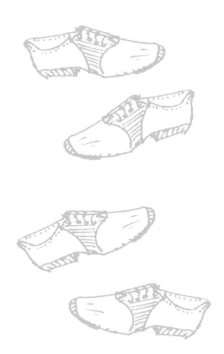

The Entertainment

This time, I totally messed up. Even though it was a smaller dinner party, I wanted to add some pizazz to the evening and make it special for Mak. I searched for a wandering band that could walk around the tables like they do in St. Tropez.

My surprise turned out to be a bit of a flop. I'm not sure whether it's because the performers weren't any good, or if the situation itself didn't work, or if my demanding and impatient husband didn't give them a chance—he told them to either get it going or get going. I finally just sent them home even though I had them booked for another hour! Luckily, we had some friends give hilarious speeches that really made the evening. The lesson: Generally, a tried and tested formula is the way to go, especially with a band. Unless you've experienced the band firsthand, it's difficult to tell whether they are good or not, even if you have watched their YouTube videos.

The formula

A birthday boy called Mak

·

Thirty of his closest friends

·

A color scheme of
gold, black, and blue

·

"Very Mak" objects from around
the house (cigars, regular sized
calculators, and gold coins).

·

Paper lanterns

·

Vodka bottles and gold vases that
resemble vodka bottles

·

Mak posters, signs, and cushions

·

Real, nougat, and bronze cigars

·

Gold-sprayed palm leaves

·

Blue and gold roses

·

Black and gold vases

·

Three jumbo calculators

AN OCTOBER DINNER

For an artsy crowd

A couple of weeks ago I dove into my garage to retrieve last year's goods – massive dried chilies wrapped in corn husks, a pile of dried fall leaves that are the perfect basis for a table runner, and copious amounts of dried orange slices. My fall rehaul came just in time to host a dinner during London Frieze Week for Adam Lindemann.

The Guest List

It was fun because the guest list he gave me was an eclectic group of art collectors, artists, and vintage car enthusiasts who also happened to be art lovers. I also added New Yorkers who knew Adam and his wife, Amalia, as well as artsy London-based individuals who either already knew the couple or I thought would be interesting for him to meet.

The Mix

Given that it was Frieze Week and there were about a hundred other parties happening that very night, I knew people would want to party hop. So, I cut myself some slack and skipped the seating plan. Instead I set up a free-for-all buffet. In a scenario like this, I hope that the guests who walk into my party are having way too much fun to leave! At some point, there were about forty guests in the house, and God knows how many filtered in and out throughout the evening!

The Food I hate fussing about party food. I went with my tried-and-true Lebanese caterers. Lebanese mezze and grills will satisfy carnivores and vegans alike, it's a no-brainer when you have a mixed bag of guests floating in and out. For dessert, my friend Peri made some of her delicious Oreo cookie mousse, and I ordered a selection of cupcakes from Lola's, which qualify as both dessert and eye candy. Huge, chewy chocolate chip cookies rounded out the menu. I had strategically strewn color coordinated candies and chocolates in each room— one of the best décor tricks in the book.

The Energy All in all, despite being a salad mix of people, it totally worked. Everyone met someone new and interesting that they wouldn't have otherwise met before, including a friend who met an artist whose work she's purchased. And that's why your guest list should be eclectic!

THE FOOTBALL (SOCCER) THEMED PARTY

Boys will be boys ...

One client of mine told me that her husband was a dedicated soccer fanatic and she wanted to create a party around this theme for his 50th birthday. I was excited to do something different—despite the fact that I knew next to nothing about soccer!

Regardless of my deficiency regarding all things soccer, I was going to get the aesthetics right. While basing a theme around a sport is very boyish, this was a black-tie party for grown ups, which made it so much fun to bring to life. The couple lived in North London and had a huge garden that we could tent and decorate, but if the die-hard soccer aficionado in your life has a big birthday coming up, the ideas we used can be rolled out whatever the size of the space you have to work with.

The tent we chose was red, with a black and white striped top. We covered the tables with Astroturf, and soccer balls made from flowers were the centerpiece arrangements. The napkins were folded to look like soccer shirts, a fun trick that added an extra touch to the theme. My favorite bit was the matching place cards and chair covers with striped fabric with the names emblazoned in yellow across the back to look like soccer jerseys. Naming the tables is another great way to keep the mood in theme and move away from the coldness of table numbers. In this case, we went for 'stands.'

And of course, a birthday cake in the shape of a soccer jersey rounded it all out.

NIG

50

HAPPY
BIRTHD

Why every party you throw should be a theme party

Having a theme party makes the occasion feel that much more special and distinguishes it as a celebration. More importantly, a theme allows you to create a backdrop against which you can choreograph your evening.

To me, themes come in two categories. The first is what springs to mind as soon as you hear the words 'theme party' uttered: costumes. The second is a matter of motif—tying the décor, table, and potentially the food and drinks to match a particular concept.

Costumed extravaganzas

There's nothing like dressing up and playing pretend for a night. The fun starts before you get there—the moment that you receive the invite, the hunt for the perfect costume begins. A good theme gives you the chance to let your imagination run a bit wild, dares you to get into character and take a break from your usual self. The cherry on top is the series of phone calls with friends to plan costumes and the shopping expeditions to various thrift/costumes stores to find essential accessories.

Themed dinner parties

Although upscale parties are nice, not every one can be a costumed. The excitement of crafting the perfect costume wears a bit thin if you have to do it more than a few times a year. This is when the motif themes become perfect for every occasion, including an intimate dinner party at home for as few as four people. For me it's all about the table décor and getting creative with it—you can carry the motif into the menu as well.

Motif themes can be based on the time of year, a person being feted, or simply a color combination. I like to set the theme from the get-go with the invitation to achieve continuity with respect to the colors and mood. Working within defined guidelines from that early on makes it easier to choose everything from décor and food to music. It keeps things streamlined and elegant, and helps maintain your sanity.

Should you have a party? The answer is YES!

(And it should be a dinner party.)

My family and friends will attest that throwing a party is my answer to almost everything. Whenever my teenage daughters have issues with their friends, I always tell them to have people over. It's a great way to bring the invitees closer together and bridge any differences. It's also a great way to punish the uninvited!

Apart from that, there are other great reasons to host a party. Here are just ten of them (Ten Reasons to Entertain) but trust me there are plenty more.

1. It's somebody's birthday!
2. To combat the Anti-Social Movement: we all spend way too much time online and don't get enough in real life interaction. And that just isn't right. The best way to wage war on this phenomenon? A party!
3. To welcome a friend or family member coming to town or to bid farewell to one who's leaving.
4. To kick off a season or to celebrate a holiday: Christmas, Thanksgiving, Diwali, Easter, Cinco de Mayo, London Fashion Week... everything is fair game.
5. Because you have a new set of plates you want to show off.
6. To set romance in motion. Parties, especially dinner parties, are one of the best, low-pressure ways to set up a couple you think would be good together. Single? A party is the perfect excuse to see someone you fancy. Playing cupid at a party is how my dad met my mom: he saw her somewhere, found out his cousin was a friend of hers, and then made his cousin host a party so she could invite my mother!
7. For career purposes. Parties can afford you and your guests with incredible networking opportunities in an environment that is enjoyable.
8. Because you're happy.
9. Because you're sad.
10. Because we all need to have more fun!

Now that I've convinced that you to host a party, the question is what kind of party should you host? Weekend brunches are nice, and lunches can be fun, but the reality is that our daily lives are packed to the brim. Between work, family, errands, and household chores, just how truly present are we during daytime hours to just relax and enjoy our friends?

My choice would always be a dinner party. With dinner parties, you have the full attention of your guests—or at least as much as you are going to get! Your guests are there the whole night, real conversations and connections can be held, and that's when the real fun comes in. So what are the things that make a dinner party great and what can you do to make yours one of those? Well, that's what this book is all about. So let's go ahead and get this party started!

© 2018 Assouline Publishing
3 Park Avenue, 27th floor
New York, NY 10016, USA
Tel: 212-989-6769   Fax: 212-647-0005

www.assouline.com
Editorial director: Esther Kremer
Art director: Paola Nauges
Designer: Vanessa Geammal
Editor: Justin O'Neill
Printed in China.
ISBN: 9781614287599